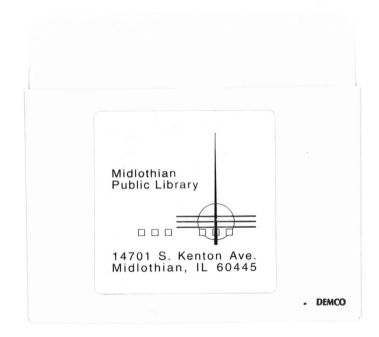

Islands

by Sheila Anderson

first step nonfiction

Lerner Publications Company · Minneapolis

What is an **island**?

It is a kind of **landform.**

An island is a piece of land
in the water.

It has water on all sides.

Islands are mountain tops
sticking up out of the water.

Some islands are **volcanoes.**

Some islands are in the
ocean.

Others are in lakes.

There are islands in rivers and **ponds.**

Boats can go around them.

Animals live on islands.

Plants grow on islands.

People live on islands.

They catch fish in the water
around the islands.

There are many things to
do on an island.

Would you like to explore an island?

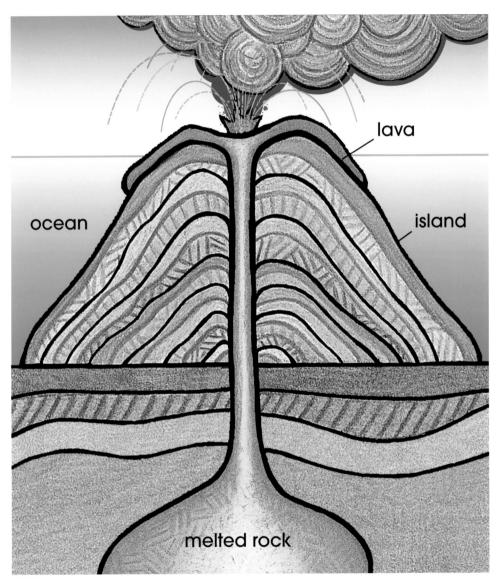

lava

island

ocean

melted rock

Volcanic Islands

Some islands are formed when volcanoes erupt under the ocean. Hot, melted rock from deep within the earth comes out of a crack in the earth's crust. It is pushed upward. When the melted rock comes out it is called lava. The lava cools. It makes a bump of new earth. More and more lava comes out, and the bump gets bigger and bigger. It becomes an underwater mountain. When the mountain gets so tall that it sticks up out of the ocean, it is an island.

Island Facts

 Many islands are formed when volcanoes erupt under the ocean.

 The Hawaiian Islands are a group of volcanic islands. They are part of the United States.

 Japan is a country in Asia. It is made up of four main islands and more than three thousand smaller islands.

The largest island in the world is Greenland. It is about three times the size of the state of Texas. More than half of Greenland is covered in ice.

Many kinds of animals live on the Galapagos Islands in South America. One of these is the giant tortoise. It can weigh more than 500 pounds and live up to 150 years!

Glossary

 island – a piece of land that has water on all sides

 landform – a natural feature of the earth's surface

 ocean - a large area of salt water that covers nearly three fourths of Earth

 ponds – bodies of water that are smaller than lakes

 volcanoes – breaks in Earth's surface where hot, melted rock called lava flows out

Index

The images in this book are used with the permission of: © Jason Hosking/Stone/Getty Images, pp. 2, 22 (top); © Gary Yeowell/Photographer's Choice/Getty Images, pp. 3, 22 (second from top); © Caroline von Tuempling/Stone/Getty Images, p. 4; © Gary Yeowell/Stone/Getty Images, p.5; © Dick Roberts/Visuals Unlimited, p. 6; © SuperStock, Inc./SuperStock, pp. 7, 22 (bottom); © Wolcott Henry/National Geographic/Getty Images, pp. 8, 22 (center); © Chip Forelli/The Image Bank/Getty Images, p. 9; © Hans Wolf/Riser/Getty Images, pp. 10, 22 (second from bottom); © age fotostock/SuperStock, p. 11; © Joel Sartore/National Geographic/Getty Images, p. 12; © Michael Cogliantry/Photonica/Getty Images, p. 13; © Wayne Walton/Lonely Planet Images/Getty Images, p. 14; © Colin Prior/Stone/Getty Images, p. 15; © Kurt Scholz/SuperStock, p. 16; © David Deas/DK Stock/Getty Images, p. 17.

Front cover: © Henry Lehn/Visuals Unlimited.

Lerner Publications Company
A division of Lerner Publishing Group, Inc.
241 First Avenue North
Minneapolis, MN 55401 U.S.A.

Website address: www.lernerbooks.com

Library of Congress Cataloging-in-Publication Data

Anderson, Sheila.
    Islands / by Sheila Anderson.
        p.   cm. — (First step nonfiction. Landforms)
    Includes index.
    ISBN: 978–0–8225–8594–7 (lib. bdg. : alk. paper)
    1. Islands—Juvenile literature. 2. Island ecology—Juvenile literature. I. Title.
GB471.A53 2008
551.42—dc22   2007007813

Manufactured in the United States of America
1 2 3 4 5 6 – DP – 13 12 11 10 09 08